Christmas
TRADITIONS

Christmas
TRADITIONS

A celebration of festive lore

George Goodwin

Contents

....

THE TRANSATLANTIC 'VICTORIAN' CHRISTMAS

CHRISTMAS AROUND THE WORLD

MODERN TRADITIONS

C

C for the Crack
That Kate
with H

D

for our Doggie
With cap on his head.

Introduction

The human need for a midwinter festival is long-standing. Centred around the shortest day, it is a time to commemorate the old year and welcome the new. In Europe, for the best part of two millennia, the celebration has had the birth of Jesus at its centre. Throughout that time the festival has been a combination of the religious and the secular, with those two elements intertwined in its rituals.

Though there have been periods when any form of celebration was discouraged, these have ultimately come to an end, for the one constant down the ages has been the desire to bring light and colour to the darkest part of the year.

> England was merry England, when
> Old Christmas brought his sports again.
> 'Twas Christmas broach'd the mightiest ale;
> 'Twas Christmas told the merriest tale.

Sir Walter Scott, 'Marmion', 1808

'C is for Cracker', from *Father Christmas*
(An illustrated rhyming alphabet), 1894

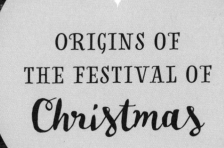

ORIGINS OF
THE FESTIVAL OF
Christmas

Roman Saturnalia

....

Saturn was the Roman god of agriculture and time. In recognising the agrarian roots of prosperity, his remit also covered wealth. His portfolio was further expanded with the gift of freedom from restraint. By the first century BC, his feast day was combined with that of his sister/wife Opis (goddess of the fruits of the earth and abundance) and also with that of the shortest day. The result was a seven-day festival (17 to 23 December) with its own greeting of 'Io Saturnalia'.

In 45 BC Julius Caesar's new Julian calendar was introduced and the shortest day of the year was declared to be, without variation, 25 December. In the following centuries, the festival period extended to include the entire period between Saturnalia and the celebration of the New Year.

Saturnalia was a time of feasting and partying, whether at home, at work or in the streets. It was a time of present-giving and licence, when sober Roman citizens would dress gaudily and also cross-dress. In houses that were lit up with candles and decorated with boughs and greenery, a junior member of the household, by accident or design, would find a bean in his slice of specially baked cake and become its Lord of Misrule. Together with his Queen of the Pea, he presided over a day of the 'world turned upside down',

(previous pages) Roberto Bompiani, *A Roman Feast*, late nineteenth century
(left) Saturn, detail from miniature attributed to Giovanni di Paolo, c. 1450

when masters served food to their servants. That last element is still echoed today, when officers in the British Armed Forces serve the other ranks at Christmas and their American equivalents do so at both Christmas and Thanksgiving.

The Roman satirist Lucian, writing in the second century AD, has Cronosolon, the priest of Cronus (Saturn) describing the festival thus: 'During my week the serious is barred; no business allowed. Drinking and being drunk, noise and games and dice, appointing of kings and feasting of slaves, singing naked, clapping of tremulous hands, an occasional ducking of corked faces in icy water – such are the functions over which I preside.'

Saturn has come down to us, with sickle or scythe, as Old Father Time and, less charmingly, as the Grim Reaper. More happily, his name has been given to Saturday, one of the most well-regarded days of the week.

A sketch of a stone relief depicting Mithras sacrificing a bull, found in Micklegate, York in 1749

The Winter Solstice and the Birth of the Unconquered Sun

The Romans could be very accommodating when it came to importing foreign gods; after all, their own principal deities, including Jupiter and Juno, as well as Saturn, were originally Greek. As the Roman Empire expanded and emperors came from the non-Italian provinces, so did a great number of gods. A short-lived attempt by the Syrian-born teenage Emperor Elagabalus to make the Sun God

Elagabal the principal deity was rejected in AD 222, along with Elagabalus himself.

However, in 274, the Emperor Aurelian was more successful in promoting the worship of the Unconquered Sun (Sol Invictus). By 354 an Invictus festival coincided with the Roman date for the winter solstice of 25 December. The date of 25 December may also have had significance in Mithraism, a highly secretive ritualised cult amongst high-ranking Roman soldiers, civil servants and merchants.

So even before Emperor Constantine the Great gave imperial support to Christianity in circa AD 323, 25 December was already long established as a significant date in the Roman calendar.

Christ's Birthday and Cristes Maesse

....

During the early years of Christianity, many different dates were given for the birth of Jesus, with the Philocalian Calendar of AD 354, produced in Rome, providing the first known record of 25 December.

It was long assumed that the choice of day was due to Emperor Constantine the Great's official support for Christianity and the early Christian leaders' policy of establishing their Church by superimposing their holy days onto major pagan festivals. However, 25 December was actually chosen because it followed exactly nine months after the more significant and earlier established date of 25 March for the Annunciation. In addition, those early Christians, far from associating themselves with heathen events, in fact deliberately sought to distance themselves from them.

It was only centuries later, when the Christian importance of 25 December was strongly established in much of continental Europe, that this attitude changed. The different approach was definitively marked when Pope Gregory the Great sent St Augustine to begin the conversion of England in 597 with the confidence that, in a converted land, the celebration of the birthday of 'the Light of the World' would become the focal point of any ongoing midwinter festival.

Incidentally, such was the significance of 25 March (or Lady Day) that it – and not 1 January – officially began the English New Year between 1155 and 1752. Lady Day's importance in the popular mind has now, of course, long been eclipsed by that of Christmas.

The word 'Christmas' comes from the Old English *Crīstes mæsse*, literally 'the Mass of Christ': Christ meaning 'the Anointed' and Mass, now obviously a service, but originally from the ecclesiastical Latin *missa* or 'dismissal'. With a forerunner in the form of a fourth-century pre-Nativity vigil in the Eastern Christian Church, a Midnight Mass was first celebrated in Rome by Pope Sixtus III (AD 432–440) and it remained a purely papal service until the mid-twelfth century, when it was performed by the priesthood more generally. From that time onward, Midnight Mass has been, for countless Christians, the first joyous celebration of the birth of Christ the Saviour that marks the real beginning of Christmas.

As for the word Xmas, far from being a modern contraction, it actually derives from the first letter of the Greek Χριστός, or 'Christos' in romanised text. It appears in the abbreviated form – then expressed as XPmas – in an *Anglo-Saxon Chronicle* entry relating to 1021, with the longer form of 'Christmas' being first used in an entry for 1038. Coinciding with expanding Norman influence during the rest of the eleventh century, 'Christmas' increasingly replaced 'Yule' as the recognised term for the midwinter festival in most of England.

Miniature by Giovan Pietro Birago from the *Sforza Hours*, 1490–1521

'Bringing Home Christmas', illustration by R. Seymour
from Thomas Hervey's *The Book of Christmas*, 1836

Yule: Lights and Evergreens

Yule, the Anglo-Saxon equivalent of the Old Norse *jöl*, was a pagan festival of the winter solstice, marking the beginning of the New Year. It was a time for dramatising the death of the old year and encouraging the bounty of the new one through fertility rites. One of these was 'wassailing', a word derived from the Old Norse *ves heill*, meaning 'be well and healthy'. The local brew would be poured onto fruit trees as well as down the throats of the wassailers.

As with the Roman Saturnalia, Yule was at midwinter, when the crops had been harvested, meat was fresh and alcohol newly brewed. It was a time for celebration and feasting. It was also when evergreens were brought into the home and decorated with lights, all-important in keeping the dark forces of the long nights at bay. Evergreen herbs such as bay and rosemary would be on display, together with a Yule log.

According to folklore, this large block of wood would burn over the festival period. The Yule log's namesake and more modern Christmas descendant is the frosted and ornamented chocolate Swiss roll that dates from the nineteenth century.

In pagan terms, decorative holly was taken to symbolise the male and ivy the female, but when northern Europe was Christianised, the holly's berries could also be taken to represent the blood of Christ and its leaves the crown of thorns.

Lords of Misrule, Wassailing and the Invention of Father Christmas

....

Christmas in the Middle Ages, in common with Ancient Rome's Saturnalia, was a time when 'the world turned upside down' and those at the bottom of the social pyramid were allowed to let off steam. It was believed that the sanctioning of Lords of Misrule at Christmas would reinforce the correct social order for the rest of the year. For that reason the Church often encouraged the promotion of choirboys as 'boy bishops' to run affairs (or run riot) from 6 December (the Feast Day of St Nicholas) to 28 December and Holy Innocents Day.

Understandably, a great number of real bishops believed that temporary excess bred permanent upset, and the practice was periodically banned. It was finally brought to an end in England with the Reformation, when King Henry VIII, now the Supreme Head of the Anglican Church, considered it an indignity against *his* authority. But in recent times, an increasing number of cathedrals and churches, particularly in England, the United States and Spain, have reinstituted the 'chorister bishops' – as they are now called where girls also qualify – but they have not given them their former powers!

Illustration by Myles Birket Foster from *Christmas with the Poets*, 1855

THE WASSAIL.

At least as early as the fourteenth century, communal drinking from a prized wassail bowl or cup was an activity of high society. By the sixteenth century, wassailing had spread to all ranks, when groups of wassailers might offer a householder a verse or two and a drink from their cup in exchange for money. However, as with the medieval performance in masks known as 'mumming', there could be a 'trick or treat' or criminal element to the custom if the householder refused to pay for these drink-related and often riotous singing and play-acting 'offerings' that were allowed a degree of licence at Christmastime.

Medieval kings were fond of having their own Kings of the Bean or Lords of Misrule. This continued into the Renaissance, with James IV of Scotland and Henry VII of England also both retaining Abbots of Unreason. Though Henry VIII stopped the parodying of his Church, he was very keen on the secular Lords of Misrule and was still ordering their creation in the final years of his reign.

The last of the English royal Lords of Misrule was in the reign of Edward VI (1547–53), though some noble houses and town corporations still continued to appoint their own afterwards. In Scotland there was one last glorious – and rare – Queen of the Bean under Mary Queen of Scots in 1564.

Mary's son and successor James VI was cautious in Scotland, but after he became James I of England in 1603, he treated Puritan disapproval with disdain and ordered his Master of the Revels to create glorious spectacles. When a play on each of the twelve days of Christmas and a masque on Twelfth Night did not sate his appetite, he ordered an additional masque on Christmas Night itself. In the hands of playwright Ben Jonson and set designer Inigo Jones, the Jacobean Christmas masque was a lavish combination of music, dance, drama, poetry, elaborate masks and costumes, all set against spectacular scenery.

In 1616, Jonson's *Christmas, His Masque* introduced Captain Christmas or Christmas of London to represent the season. The fifteenth-century carol 'Sir Christèmas' preceded Jonson in personifying Christmas, but Jonson's was a rounded and burlesque figure of fun who entered the festivities with his ten children. Their names identify many of the celebratory elements of the Christmas period that were then familiar and that the Puritans denounced. They were: Misrule, Carol, Mince Pie, Gambol, Post and Pair,* New Year's Gift, Mumming, Wassail, Offering and Baby Cake.

The character of Christmas, increasingly called Father Christmas, made a greater number of appearances after this time. In 1638, in another court masque, Christmas was presented as 'an old reverend gentleman in furred gown and cap'. Yet, soon afterwards, he was forced to go into hiding. For during the 1640s and 1650s the political world really was turned upside down: puritanical 'Godly Rule' took hold and Father Christmas and his 'children' were outlawed.

* A card game.

Sint Nikolaas laat door uw schoorsteen glijden,
Heel korven lekkers, om u te verblijden.
't Is zeker dat, bij 't zien dier schoone dingen,
Ge hem danken zult, en ook van vreugd zult springen.

Par les tuyaux de votre cheminée,
Saint Nicolas viendra vous apporter

St Nicholas and Sinterklaas

The name Santa Claus is an Anglicisation of Sinterklaas, a Dutch form of St Nicholas. This St Nicholas, a fourth-century Bishop of Myra, was so venerated by the eleventh century that he became one of the victims of the medieval practice of 'saint stealing'. His body was disinterred in 1087 and taken to Bari in southern Italy, where it remains to this day.

Bari profited greatly as a place of pilgrimage as St Nicholas's remit continued to grow. He is the patron saint of a number of countries (including Greece and Russia), and has Amsterdam, New York and Liverpool among his cities. With an eye to his future role, it is notable that his bulging medieval portfolio included merchants and all children. He was also said to protect sailors, for whom he flew over stormy seas to calm them. Either 5 December, the eve of St Nicholas's feast day, or the day itself was widely celebrated across medieval Europe as a time for delivering presents into the stockings and shoes of good children, and for leaving the birch rod for naughty ones.

With St Nicholas being celebrated as Sinterklaas in the Netherlands, it was once wrongly assumed that seventeenth-century Dutch settlers in New Amsterdam, the forerunner of New York, had taken the tradition to North America. In fact it would be nineteenth-century New Yorkers who both established the legend of Sinterklaas in America and ultimately transformed him into Santa Claus.

Sint Nikolaas, anonymous late nineteenth-century Dutch print

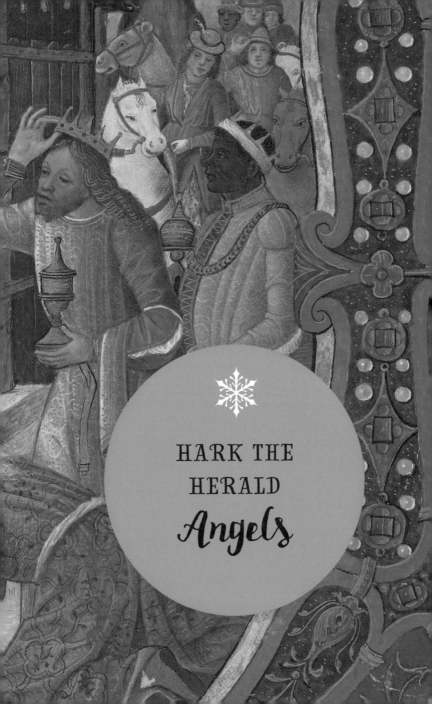

HARK THE
HERALD
Angels

The Christmas Crib
and Nativity Play

Though brought together in many of Renaissance art's magnificent 'Adorations of Christ', the shepherds and the Three Wise Men, or Magi, do not actually appear together in the Gospels: the Wise Men of Matthew Chapter II arrive on Epiphany, the day after the twelfth night of the Christmas season, which is long after the visit of the shepherds recounted in Luke Chapter II. Also, as part of the depiction of the Christmas story, it is just an assumption that sheep accompanied the shepherds to the manger and that there they joined the stable animals, including oxen and asses (donkeys), at the birthplace of the child who would become the Good Shepherd of John's Gospel.

According to his thirteenth-century biographer, St Francis of Assisi was the creator of the first visual celebration of the Christmas crib – or manger – in 1223. The crib in Greccio, Italy, was certainly centre stage in St Francis's own Nativity play, but it would, perhaps, be better to describe St Francis as the refiner and populariser rather than the creator of the tradition, as it has been discovered that other churches had singing and dancing around a crib for more than a century before St Francis's service at Greccio. However, in spite of

(previous pages) *Adoration of the Magi*, miniature, c. 1500

(left) Giotto, *Institution of the Crib at Greccio*, fresco from the Basilica of St Francis in Assisi, 1297–1300

such simple beginnings, the tradition of the Christmas crib and the Nativity play have both grown.

The Christmas crib or Nativity scene became popular in Catholic Europe during the succeeding centuries. In Italy, homes as well as churches continue to display these ornamental *presepi*. In England, however, only since the beginning of the twentieth century have Nativity scenes become more common in English homes and churches, where they are the focus for child-friendly crib-dedication services on Christmas Eve.

Another child-focused service is Christingle. Based around strong visual images such as the lighting of individual Christingle candles held in oranges that represent Christ as 'the light of the world', this service was created in the Moravian Church in Germany in 1747. Once again it has only recently become well known and popular in the UK since being introduced into the Church of England at Lincoln Cathedral in 1968.

Far more ancient are the English roots of the Nativity play. Even before St Francis's service in 1223, the Christmas story was being dramatised for English congregations that did not understand Latin. By the thirteenth century, English words were being used in the dramas. Also, as with the Easter plays and the Mystery (or Miracle) plays at the Feast of Corpus Christi (sixty days after Easter), everyday elements took on a more prominent role.

As the secularism and the very size and complexity of these dramas increased, so did the distance between them and the altar. The players, no longer Church canons, were first moved into Church precincts and then into town squares. The biblical dramas' appeal to the common people sustained them during the early years of the Reformation, but they were far less popular with the authorities, who feared the rowdiness of the crowd. They seem to have been rarely performed from the 1570s until their revival in the twentieth century.

However, a combination of the nineteenth-century religious revival and the redefinition of Christmas as a family festival led to the recreation of the Nativity play in the UK and its counterpart, the Christmas pageant, in North America.

Today, the Nativity play is established as one of the highlights of the year in British infant schools. However, in the age-long see-sawing between the sacred and secular, some schools have changed the nature of their December plays in recent years, by adding new characters to the usual cast or, more fundamentally, by adapting the concept to give it a more secular focus.

The Christmas Carol

....

Our first Christmas carols derived from early medieval French dances based on sung verses and refrains, but their festive nature often looked back to the Anglo-Saxon Yule. This is perfectly captured in the first known English example, 'Seignors, ore entendez a nus', which dates to the early thirteenth-century time of King John. It exhorts everyone to keep open house and to be ready to ply a neighbour with drink 'until he nods his head and sleeps by day' and is written in Norman French until the final Anglo-Saxon call of '*Waesseyl!*' and response of '*Drincheyl!*' Its concentration on festive fun means it has more in common with modern songs like 'The Christmas Song' (often better known by its subtitle 'Chestnuts Roasting on an Open Fire') than with 'O Come, All Ye Faithful' and other hymns of praise, though its sense of collective communal celebration makes it as much a carol as 'The Boar's Head Carol', the more directly religious 'God Rest You Merry, Gentlemen' and others that originally date from the later medieval and early modern period.

Nowadays it is far easier to make a distinction between modern Christmas songs and traditional carols than it is between those carols and hymns, with the latter proving standard favourites for outdoor carol singing as well as for indoor church services from Advent onwards. Indeed, in

Monks singing, miniature from a Book of Hours, c. 1450–60

popular terms, Christmas hymns are no longer viewed as distinct from carols.

The first directly religious English carol owes something to St Francis of Assisi. It was his order of friars who helped to develop the Italian *lauda*. This, like the first French *carole*, was a type of dance song, but now with a religious message, and it was an unknown English Franciscan friar who wrote 'A child is boren amonges man' [sic], at some point before 1350.

Using the wider definition of 'carol' to include hymns, the words of most of the best known come from two distinct periods of composition. The first was in the fifteenth and early sixteenth centuries, and the second stemmed from the Methodism of the eighteenth century and the Anglo-Catholic revival of the nineteenth. It is from that second period that most of the modern favourites come, though one can see a clear difference in approach between the likes of Charles Wesley's triumphal 'Hark the Herald Angels Sing' and the softer, more sentimental tones of the later 'Once in Royal David's City' and 'Away in a Manger', with their emphasis on the Nativity scene and baby Jesus.

Carol Singing and the Carol Service

....

In medieval England groups of watchmen were licensed to play musical instruments in order to signal their presence and thus reassure the local inhabitants. Some of these 'waits' were often renowned for their singing. By the first decades of the nineteenth century their role had been reduced and they were only specifically licensed as visiting musicians at Christmas who collected their money from householders on Boxing Day.

The American writer Washington Irving, in the 'Christmas Eve' chapter of his *The Sketch Book of Geoffrey Crayon, Gent* (1819–20) gives us a wonderfully evocative and idyllic description of the waits during Jane Austen's time, when Irving himself was living in England:

> I had scarcely got into bed when a strain of music seemed to break forth in the air just below the window. I listened, and found it proceeded from a band which I concluded to be the Waits from some neighbouring village. They went round the house, playing under the windows. I drew aside the curtains to hear them more distinctly. The moonbeams fell through the upper part of the casement, partially lighting up the antiquated apartment. The sounds, as they receded, became more soft and aerial, and seemed to accord with the quiet and the moonlight. I listened and listened – they became more tender and remote, and, as

they gradually died away, my head sunk upon the pillow, and
I fell asleep.

Irving's depiction was far from being a universal
experience. In theory the waits were the sober
counterparts of the unlicensed and often unruly wassailers
and mummers. Things were often very different in practice,
with an early copy of *Punch* magazine declaring: 'Carols are
never entirely satisfactory when suggestive of frequent visits
to a public house.'

By the time of Irving's description, the waits were already
dying out in many parts of the country and, with them,
Christmas carolling. The latter, however, did revive and did
so as part of the great hymn-singing revival. Carol singing
was taken indoors into churches, with extraordinary
success, after Edward White Benson, Bishop of Truro and
later Archbishop of Canterbury, created the Festival of Nine
Lessons and Carols in 1880. Benson's aim was to persuade
the locals to leave the pubs, with their rowdy singalongs
and bawdy behaviour, in favour of more wholesome and
decorous singing in church, and in this he was spectacularly
successful.

The Nine Lessons and Carols became popular all over
the country and the remaining waits and the traditional
village carollers were no more. There were still carol singers
going house to house in the twentieth century, but these

'They went round the house, playing under the windows', illustration
by Cecil Aldin from Washington Irving's *Sketch Book*, 1910 edition

tended to be small groups of children and from the 1980s onwards the practice rather fell away. Carol singers now sing to raise money for charities, rather than for themselves, and do so in places such as town squares and outside stations and supermarkets.

The most famous rendering of the Nine Lessons and Carols, the quintessential Christmas carol service, is on Christmas Eve afternoon at King's College Chapel, Cambridge. It was first given in 1918 and the practice of a single chorister singing the first verse of 'Once in Royal David's City' was introduced the following year. With just one early exception, the service at King's has been broadcast by the BBC every year since 1928 and can be heard at various times over Christmas on more than 300 American local radio stations.

'A Festival of Nine Lessons and Carols in King's College Chapel, Cambridge, England, on Christmas Eve', City of Birmingham School of Printing, 1936

Epiphany and the Three Wise Men

The 1823 publication entitled *Christmas Gambols, and Twelfth Night's Amusements* explained the importance of Epiphany on 6 January, which marks the end of the Christmas season.

> Epiphany is a *Greek* word, signifying an appearance of light, a manifestation. And this Festival is kept to celebrate the Manifestation of our Lord and Saviour JESUS CHRIST to the Gentiles. It has a particular reference to the Wise Men of the East, who were directed in a supernatural manner, by a Star, to leave their own country, and come into Judea, to enquire after our Saviour and pay him homage. Herod, the King, directed them to Bethlehem; and upon their leaving Jerusalem, the same Star which they saw in the East, went before them, and at last stood over the place where the young Child was. The house being pointed out, they went into it, fell down, and worshipped the HOLY ONE, and opening their treasures, presented unto him, gold, frankincense [burnt as incense] & myrrh [used in perfume and incense].

A Greek manuscript of the fifth century AD gave the Wise Men's names as Gathaspa, Melchior and Bithisarea, which are strikingly similar to the most common modern form of Caspar, Melchior and Balthazar.

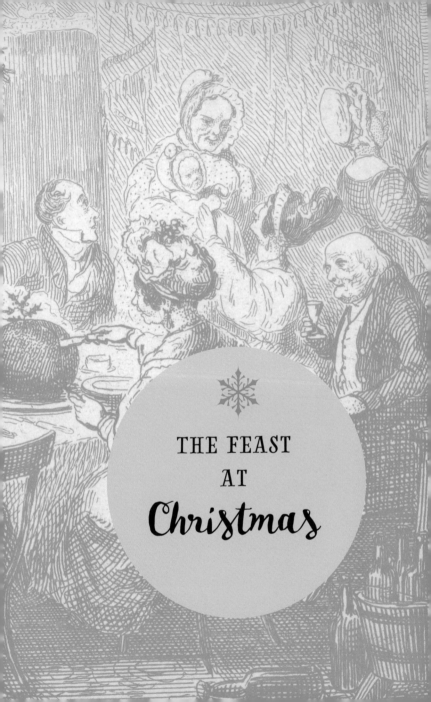

THE FEAST
AT
Christmas

The Twelve Days of Christmas

It was the Council of Tours of 567 AD that decreed a religious holiday for the entire twelve-day period from Christ's Nativity on 25 December to the eve of Epiphany. Fasting was banned, though that was balanced with the Council's injunction that there would be forty days of contemplation and fasting beforehand. This earlier period would become known as St Martin's Lent and was the forerunner of Advent. In the perennial tussle between commemoration and overcelebration, subsequent Councils reintroduced fasting days around the New Year with the aim of checking bucolic excess.

In England, the twelve-day celebration was given legal recognition in 877 AD by Alfred the Great, even before the winter festival was known as Christmas.

Aside from Christmas Day itself, the principal days of the festival in common across the Western Christian church are: 26 December (for St Stephen, the first Christian martyr); 27 December (for St John the Evangelist); 28 December (the Day of Holy Innocents); and 6 January (Epiphany). Since 1931, 1 January has been celebrated throughout the Roman Catholic Church as the Solemnity of Mary, the Holy Mother of God, while the Church of England and other churches such as the Episcopalian and Lutheran continue to commemorate it as Jesus's naming day.

As for the rhyme 'The Twelve Days of Christmas', all kinds of explanations have been offered for the words, but a simple one is given in the *Oxford Dictionary of Nursery Rhymes*. Deriving from an original French chant, the English version, first published in around 1780, was presented as just a highly imaginative memory-and-forfeits game in a children's book called *Mirth without Mischief*. That said, having provided more than two centuries of festive fun, it deserves its place as a Christmas illustration.

(previous pages) 'Christmas Dinner', illustration by R. Seymour from Thomas Hervey's *The Book of Christmas*, 1836

'A Partridge in a Pear Tree' from *The Twelve Days of Christmas*, 1780

Twelfth Night

For Dickens and his Victorian contemporaries, Twelfth Night, or the eve of Epiphany, was the final night of the Christmas season and one of the highlights of the entire festival of Christmas. It is now stripped of its former importance and displaced by New Year's Eve as the night of major revelry. As the years go by, even its sole surviving ritual – the taking down of decorations – is less often observed. The night itself has long ceased to echo Shakespeare's Twelfth Night, but many of its traditions still exist, though taking place on other days of the Christmas season and often in altered form.

Such Twelfth Night traditions had pagan elements, for instance the cross-dressing of pantomime, harking back not only to Shakespeare's play and the Jacobean masque but all the way to Saturnalia. The Christmas cake of today used to be a Twelfth Night cake in Dickens's day and, like Ancient Rome's Saturnalia cake, it would create a King of the Bean and a Queen of the Pea for those who found the hidden pulses baked in it. Whereas the Christian commemoration of Epiphany moved forward to the Sunday after 6 January, the more pagan-derived elements of Twelfth Night gradually moved backwards in the calendar, to begin either in December or to be celebrated on individual days in that month. Twelfth Night's more Bacchanalian elements have now been integrated into the modern-day New Year's Eve celebrations.

'Twelfth Night Merry Making in Farmer Shakeshaft's Barn', illustration by Hablot Knight Browne for William Harrison Ainsworth's *Mervyn Clitheroe*, 1858

Twelfth Night, as a peak time for celebration in early seventeenth-century England, was perhaps best captured in the poem 'Twelfe-Night, or King and Queene' in Robert Herrick's *Hesperides*, with its first line of 'Now, now the mirth comes'. Although written in 1648 as a backward-looking protest against Puritan restrictions, it celebrates the traditional elements of the feast.

The Puritan Christmas and After

The Puritan approach to Christmas is admirably summed up by the Pilgrim Father William Bradford. In this modernised version of his last diary entry for 1621, he describes how a group of new arrivals to the Plymouth Colony were not attuned to proper principles. He gives himself his designated title of 'the Governor' in what follows:

On the day called Christmas Day, the Governor called all to work (as was usual), but most of this new company excused themselves and said it went against their consciences to work on that day. So the Governor told them that if they made it a matter of conscience, he would spare them till they were better informed. So he led away the rest and left them; but when the workers came home at noon from their work, he found the others in the street openly at play; some pitching the bar* and some at stoolball† and such like sports. So he went to them, and took away their implements, and told them that it was against *his* conscience that they should play and others work. If they made keeping the day a matter of devotion, let them keep to their houses, but there should be no gaming or revelling in the streets.

* Log-hurling or tossing the caber.
† An ancestor of both cricket and baseball.

(right) *The Vindication of Christmas*, pamphlet, 1653

The Vindication of
CHRISTMAS,
OR,
His Twelve Yeares Observations upon the

Times, concerning the lamentable Game called Sweep-
stake ; acted by General *Plunder*, and Major General *Tax*;
With his Exhortation to the people ; a description of that
oppressing Ringworm called *Excize* ; and the manner how
our high and mighty Christmas-Ale that formerly would
knock down *Hercules*, & trip up the heels of a Giant, strook
into a deep Consumption with a blow from *Westminster*.

Since which time nothing has been attempted in that way, *at least openly* [author's italics].

Christmas did not become an official holiday in Massachusetts until 1856.

Across the Atlantic, the 1643 'Solemn League and Covenant', which united the English and Scottish Parliaments against Charles I, introduced religious changes that would further 'Godly Rule'. On 19 December 1644, Christmas was singled out in particular 'to be kept with the more solemn humiliation, because it may call to remembrance our sins, and the sins of our forefathers, who have turned this Feast, pretending the memory of Christ into an extreme forgetfulness of him, by giving liberty to carnal and sensual delights'.

Parliament's actions created great resentment, as is made clear both in 'Hue and Cry After Christmas' and 'The Vindication of Christmas', two secretly printed anti-Puritan pamphlets.

Oliver Cromwell has been wrongly accused of 'abolishing' Christmas, as the 1644 measures were passed when he was a leading military figure rather than the dominant political one. As a religious Independent, he was less dogmatic about uniformity of religious practice. At the same time, he did not remove the restrictions on Christmas celebrations when he became politically pre-eminent. He and his regime of major generals knew that large numbers of people coming together in outdoor festive celebration could rapidly lead, deliberately or spontaneously, to violent protest. That said, neither Parliament nor Cromwell, as is sometimes alleged, specifically proscribed Christmas pudding or mince pies. The supposed 'ban' is as much a myth as the claim that such edibles were still off the menu until King George I – erroneously and bizarrely described as 'the Pudding King' – personally brought them back.

Christmas was reprieved in England on the return of Charles II in 1660. Though there was not a full restoration of what had gone before, there was certainly a revival by the 1720s, if the impressions of the English at Christmas by the wealthy Swiss visitor, César-François de Saussure, are taken to be generally true:

> They wish each other a Merry Christmas and a Happy New Year, presents are given, and no one may dispense with this custom. On this festival day churches, the entrance of houses, rooms, kitchens, and halls are decked with laurels, rosemary, and other greenery. Everyone from the King to the artisan eats soups and Christmas pies. The soup is called Christmas porridge, and is a dish few foreigners find to their taste. I must describe it to you, for it will amuse you. You must stew dried raisins, plums, and spice in broth, rich people add wine and others beer, and it is a great treat for English people, but, I assure you, not for me. As to Christmas pies, everyone likes them, and they are made with chopped meat, currants, beef-suet, and other good things. You never taste these dishes except for two or three days before and after Christmas, and I cannot tell you the reason why.

The Origins of Turkey, Plum Pudding and Mince Pies

The trophy Christmas dish of the medieval king's table, and of many a table down the social hierarchy, was the boar's head. Its traditional prominence looked back to Anglo-Saxon Yule and continued well after its Tudor celebration in the 'Boar's Head Carol'. But it had long been displaced among the population as a whole by the time that Washington Irving was honouring it in his fictional description of Christmas Day in his *Sketch Book* of 1819–20.

Roast beef and plum pudding were then the national dishes of a true-born Englishman and thus the festival food of celebration, both at Christmas and at other times of the year. They were the wholesome chosen food that differentiated the English from the 'weedy' French, who were portrayed as eating frogs' legs in good times and grass in bad.

The nineteenth-century Christmas alternative to beef, particularly in the south of England, was goose. As a more expensive choice, there was also turkey; indeed, turkey had been available in England since the sixteenth century and in a 1573 poem was approvingly described as 'Christmas husbandlie fare'. By the eighteenth century turkeys were already being reared in numbers in Norfolk

'A Poulterer's Shop, Holborn Hill', from *A Holiday Book for Christmas and the New Year*, 1852

and Cambridgeshire, as they were popular with the well-to-do. Turkeys were herded towards London from August onwards with small leather boots to protect their feet.

Turkey's presumed superiority to goose in the 1840s is made clear in Dickens's *A Christmas Carol*, when the reformed Scrooge sends Bob Cratchit an enormous turkey for his family's Christmas dinner. However, Britain did not begin to catch up with America in making turkey commonplace and the dominant choice at Christmas until the expansion of refrigeration in the 1950s.

Plum pudding had its origins in plum[b] pottage, a medieval bread-and-boiled-meat porridge that was served at the beginning of the meal. By the early eighteenth century the pottage also contained other dried fruit and was flavoured with spices, sugar and wine. Deemed unpopular with foreigners, it lost favour even with the British during the next half century.

Pottage's demise and pudding's rise can be charted through the pages of three well-known eighteenth-century cookbooks. Pottage and not pudding is included in Eliza Smith's 1727 *The Compleat Housewife*. There are recipes for both in Hannah Glasse's 1746 *The Art of Cookery Made Plain and Easy*, with that for pottage almost the same as Smith's, but its title, 'To Make Plumb Porridge for Christmas', highlights it as merely a seasonal dish. By the time of Charlotte Mason's 1773 *The Ladies' Assistant*, the pottage

'Puddings and Pastries', illustration from *Mrs Beeton's Book of Household Management*, 1892

Open Apple Tart.   Galette.

Iced Pudding.

Apricot Fritters.

Pancakes & Apricot Jam.

Charlotte Russe.

Macaroni Cheese.

Cherry Tart.

Mince Pies.

Almond Puddings.

Tartlets.

Compote of Fruits.

Fruit Pudding.

Fruit Tart.

Christmas Plum Pudding.

Milk Pudding.

Roly-Poly Jam Pudding.

recipe has gone, whereas the one for pudding, near identical to that of Hannah Glasse, is very similar to the one we know today. Thus there was no beef – except for suet, and no prunes – with 'plum' having become a generic name for all dried fruit – while eggs, milk, flour and brandy had been added.

Plum pudding began to take its modern 'cannonball' shape and its topping of holly by the 1830s – though fluted versions continued – and it was seen by Dickens as being central to the Christmas family feast in his 1836 *Sketches by Boz*. Yet its Christmas prefix came later, being first printed as such in Eliza Acton's aptly named 1845 *Modern Cookery*.

Modern supermarkets annually vie with each other to produce 'luxury' examples, with unusual ingredients added to the standard recipe, but by far the greatest change of recent years has been in the time saved in cooking; a shop-bought version's minutes in the microwave replaces hours of preparation and boiling. The microwaving has also put a permanent end to the tradition of inserting a coin in the pudding – a nineteenth- and twentieth-century equivalent of creating a King of the Bean.

Mince pies were first mentioned in the early seventeenth century. Like plum pottage and plum pudding, they originally contained minced meat as well as dried fruit. The myth that they were banned during the Interregnum (1649–60) arose because of known Puritan disapproval of what they regarded as the 'Romish' and 'idolatrous' practice of making the larger pies in a manger shape and adding a baby Jesus in pastry.

Kissing Under the Mistletoe

. . . .

Mistletoe's appeal as a decorative winter evergreen is straightforward. It is vibrantly alive, with its striking green leaves and white berries standing out in the dormant winter landscape. It is mentioned in the Norse myth 'The Death of Baldur' as providing the wood of the arrow that kills the god of that name, with the arrow's potency magnified by

'To the imminent peril of all the pretty housemaids', illustration from Washington Irving's *Old Christmas and Bracebridge Hall*, 1918 edition

mistletoe's poisonous nature, and it was used by Druids in pagan ceremonies.

Perhaps because of these antecedents, a myth has arisen that mistletoe has been banned in churches for many centuries; but there is no foundation for that idea. Indeed, mistletoe as a Christmas decoration is not even mentioned in literature until Robert Herrick's 1648 *Hesperides* poem on Candlemas Eve. Candlemas is on 2 February, forty days after Christmas, and was seen as the time to remove any evergreen decoration that may have outlasted Twelfth Night and Twelfth Day.

Perhaps surprisingly, the first known image of kissing under the mistletoe is a riotous cartoon of 1794, and the tradition was probably invented at some point during the eighteenth century. There is certainly no mention of 'kissing' in the comprehensive 1719–20 books on mistletoe and its uses by the apothecary Sir John Colbatch; and Washington Irving felt the need to explain 'the tradition' in a footnote to his *Sketch Book* descriptions of Christmas at Bracebridge Hall.

Whatever the provenance, its use for 'kissing' was soon much illustrated. Thus the central focus of mistletoe in the illustration of Mr Fezziwig's Christmas ball in Dickens's *A Christmas Carol* (1843) is matched by its noticeable deployment on the left-hand side.

'Mr Fezziwig's Ball', illustration by John Leech from Dickens's *A Christmas Carol*, 1843

THE
TRANSATLANTIC
'VICTORIAN'
Christmas

Washington Irving and the Revival of Christmas

The vigour of England's Christmas celebrations did not fully return after 1660 and Charles II's Restoration. Samuel Pepys tells us in his diary entry for 25 December 1666 that he went to church and enjoyed a mince pie, but he also reports that he sometimes also went into the office on Christmas Day.

In the eighteenth century and at the turn of the nineteenth, the bulk of the festivity centred around Twelfth Night and Twelfth Day, with Jane Austen, for one, enjoying home 'entertainments' such as 'theatricals' and bobbing for apples. The importance of Twelfth Night would dim and that of Christmas Day would rise during the nineteenth century.

That our own image of a 'traditional' English Christmas includes stagecoaches in the snow owes much to Charles Dickens and to Washington Irving, the American author almost thirty years Dickens's senior and someone the latter greatly admired in much the same way as Irving himself revered Walter Scott.

Irving lived in England between 1815 and 1820 and it was during that time, in 1819–20, that his *Sketch Book of Geoffrey*

(previous pages) 'R is for Reindeer', from *Father Christmas (An illustrated rhyming alphabet)*, 1894

(left) 'The little beings were as busy about him as the mock fairies about Falstaff', illustration by Cecil Aldin from Washington Irving's *Sketch Book*, 1910 edition

Crayon was published on both sides of the Atlantic to rapturous acclaim. It not only contains his famous American stories 'Rip Van Winkle' and 'Sleepy Hollow', but also his fictional Christmas at Bracebridge Hall in rural Yorkshire with the old-fashioned and genial Squire Bracebridge. *The Sketch Book*'s American tales are rightly famous, but it is the British series that has had an even greater lasting impact, because in these Irving created the very archetype of the 'traditional' English Christmas in the countryside. At a time of economic downturns but still unchecked urbanisation, with consequent social change and dislocation and the fear of increasing lawlessness on the city streets, Irving's creation of an idealised world captured the imagination of the print-buying public with an impact comparable to the 'forget your cares' Hollywood movies of the troubled 1930s.

Irving depicted a vast number of celebratory elements of Christmas – historic and archaic as well as current – in a comforting and overall harmonious setting that retained elements of fading grandeur, which in themselves authenticated the impression of long-standing seasonal festivity. Irving deliberately captured the spirit of Sir Roger de Coverley, the forerunner of both his own and Dickens's country Christmas hosts. Sir Roger, the fictional country squire in Joseph Addison and Richard Steele's *Spectator* of a hundred years before, had been depicted as somewhat unfashionable even then, but also as good natured and benevolent. He was someone who at Christmas loved 'to see the whole Village merry in my Great Hall' and who said that over its twelve days, for 'everyone that calls for it, I have always a piece of cold beef and mince pie upon the table'. Sir Roger also recounts with glee how a rigid Puritan visitor seemingly forgot his principles and ate 'very plentifully of his plum-porridge'.

But Irving's Christmas at Bracebridge Hall is a far fuller portrait of the season than that in *The Spectator*. His description is a triumphant masterpiece of recreated and even invented tradition. Irving set the tone and he and his many imitators, including Dickens in all his brilliance, established the Christmas story and with it the ideal of Christmastime.

Irving's images had extraordinary appeal in the 1820s and many of them still do. Along with the now discarded wassail bowl and wooden yule log, this is a Christmas of crackling fires, of gleaming white snow on the ground, and of the red counterpoint of robins and holly berries. This is a Christmas of conviviality and of carols, decorations and presents. Irving even has Squire Bainbridge's friend, the parson, denouncing puritanism in his sermon and instructing his congregation to enjoy themselves. Tellingly, this is a child-friendly time, of continuing young joy and laughter.

The way that Christmas was observed was changing.

Irving's Flying Sinterklaas

....

Washington Irving was also responsible for initiating a new and magical element of Christmastime. In 1809 he had created the prototype for the modern Santa Claus in his *A History of New York,* which parodied the efforts of some well-intentioned members of the New-York Historical Society, who sought to create a backlog of tradition for the vastly expanding city. Irving did this so successfully that Walter Scott – after reading it aloud to his wife and two friends – wrote that 'our sides have been absolutely sore with laughing'.

   In his history of the city, Irving created a St Nicholas who directed the early Dutch colonists to settle Manhattan when the saint was 'riding over the tops of the trees, in that self-same wagon wherein he brings his yearly presents to children'. The naturally grateful colonists thanked their guardian with the ceremony of 'hanging up a stocking in the chimney on St Nicholas Eve; which stocking is always found in the morning miraculously filled; for the good St Nicholas has ever been a great giver of gifts, particularly to children'. For this St Nicholas – capable of 'riding jollily among the treetops, or over the roofs of houses, now and then drawing forth magnificent presents from his breeches pockets, and dropping them down the chimneys' – was a

Illustration by W. W. Denslow from Clement Clarke Moore's
'A Visit from St Nicholas', 1902

Illustration by Arthur Rackham from Clement Clarke Moore's
'A Visit from St Nicholas', 1931

friend to the young. In fact he was completely child-centred, 'confining his presents merely to the children, in token of the degeneracy of the parents'!

Irving's St Nicholas was now an overall benevolent figure and, rather like Squire Bainbridge, was the personification of goodwill, though at that stage St Nicholas was still anchored to his own Saint's Day in early December. But Irving was also aware of another figure, not Dutch but English, who was the personification of Christmas itself. It is striking that, at the very beginning of the Christmas chapters in his *Sketch Book*, Irving included an epigraph taken from the 1646 anti-Puritan pamphlet 'Hue and Cry After Christmas', that reads: 'But is old, old, good old Christmas gone? Nothing but the hair of his good, gray old head and beard left? Well, I will have that, seeing I cannot have more of him.'

It would be another half-century before the jolly St Nicholas/Santa Claus figure would become one with Father Christmas, but Irving had begun the process. *The Sketch Book* rapidly became a runaway bestseller on both sides of the Atlantic and established itself as an ongoing gift at Christmastime. Other authors rapidly followed with their own Christmas stories, because they knew there was an eager audience for the type of writing that projected this new interpretation of Christmas – one that was child-friendly and homely and was securely and comfortingly based on traditions that were either long-standing or, at least, seemed to be.

Old SANTECLAUS with much delight
His reindeer drives this frosty night,
O'er chimney tops, and tracks of snow,
To bring his yearly gifts to you.

'Old Santeclaus With Much Delight'

Between Washington Irving's creation of a flying Sinterklaas and Clement Clarke Moore's ever-popular new version of St Nicholas, there was an intervening stage. A red-coated and long-white-bearded Santa was illustrated for the first time in a poem with the first line 'Old Santeclaus with Much Delight', which was published in New York in 1821 with the formal title *The Children's Friend, Number III: A New-Year's present, to the little ones from five to twelve*. Both its author and illustrator were anonymous, but, importantly, not only does Santeclaus have a name close to the modern-day version, but he is now delivering his presents on Christmas Eve rather than St Nicholas's Day and doing so personally, by taking them down the chimney and putting them in stockings. He also has a reindeer-powered sleigh, though with just the one reindeer. The scene in the accompanying verses, if not in the illustrations, is most definitely the snowy one we have come to expect.

Still to come, though, are his chubbiness and his joviality. In that latter regard Santeclaus is still very much the pre-Irving traditional figure, because, for naughty children, he brings only the birch. More than that, he is strict and forbidding, definitely believing that children should be seen but not heard.

The Children's Friend. Number III: A New-Year's Present, to the little ones from five to twelve, 1821

Old SANTECLAUS with much delight
His reindeer drives this frosty night,
O'er chimney tops, and tracks of snow,
To bring his yearly gifts to you.

The steady friend of virtuous youth,
The friend of duty, and of truth,
Each Christmas eve he joys to come
Where love and peace have made their home.

Through many houses he has been,
And various beds and stockings seen;
Some, white as snow, and neatly mended,
Others, that seem'd for pigs intended.

To some I gave a pretty doll,
To some a peg-top, or a ball;
No crackers, cannons, squibs, or rockets,
To blow their eyes up, or their pockets.

Where e'er I found good girls or boys,
That hated quarrels, strife and noise,
I left an apple, or a tart,
Or wooden gun, or painted cart;

No drums to stun their Mother's ear,
Nor swords to make their sisters fear;
But pretty books to store their mind
With knowledge of each various kind.

The Children's Friend. Number III: A New-Year's Present, to the little ones from five to twelve, 1821

But where I found the children naughty,
In manners rude, in temper haughty,
Thankless to parents, liars, swearers,
Boxers, or cheats, or base tale-bearers,

I left a long, black, birchen rod,
Such as the dread command of GOD
Directs a Parent's hand to use
When virtue's path his sons refuse.

Charles Dickens and Christmas Cheer

....

In the first exchange of letters of mutual admiration between Washington Irving and Charles Dickens, the latter conveyed just how much he would have liked to travel with Irving to Bracebridge Hall. In fact, Dickens had, as close as fiction would allow, already gone there with *The Pickwick Papers*. The Pickwickians' Christmas at Dingley Dell as the guests of Mr Wardle, the jovial local squire, owed a very great deal to Irving – as Dickens was delighted to tell him. *Pickwick*, first published in 1837, was, like Irving's *Sketch Book*, a runaway bestseller. It again successfully created the image of an ideal country Christmas of long tradition and confirmed its place in the public imagination from that time to this – as shown every year on Christmas cards.

However, there was a major change in the context of the two books: Christmas, in the short space of time between their publication, had begun to establish itself strongly as a family-friendly, domestic event. Even by the mid-1830s there were books explaining the 'true nature' of this supposedly long-standing aspect of Christmas. One such, from 1836, was Thomas K. Hervey's *The Book of Christmas*. Its subtitle, 'Descriptive of the customs, ceremonies, traditions, superstitions, fun, feeling and festivities of the Christmas Season' was comprehensive. Its illustrations by Robert

'Scrooge's Third Visitor', illustration by John Leech from Dickens's
A Christmas Carol, 1843

Seymour, who would be the initial illustrator of *Pickwick*, captured the new, idealised image of Christmas, just as a young Dickens himself did in 'Christmas Festivities', which was first published in December of the same year.

The whole season was now reanimated for those who could afford it. That spirit was captured in a supremely effervescent piece on Twelfth Night in *Leigh Hunt's London Journal*, from 1835:

Christmas goes out in fine style, with Twelfth Night. It is a finish worthy of the time. Christmas Day was the morning of the season; New Year's Day the middle of it, or Noon; Twelfth Night is the night, brilliant with innumerable planets of twelfth-cakes. The whole island keeps court; nay all Christendom. All the world are kings and queens. Everybody is somebody else, and learns at once to laugh at, and to tolerate characters different from his own, by enacting them. Cakes, characters, forfeits, lights, theatres, merry rooms, little holiday faces, and last not least, the painted sugar on the cakes, so bad to eat but so fine to look at.

The 'little holiday faces' are particularly worth noting for this acknowledgement of the importance of the entire Christmas season for children and their families. Twelfth Night was a favourite time for Dickens and his own young family, heightened by it also being the birthday of Charley, Dickens's eldest son. It was a time for recitations, songs, dancing and even conjuring. As the children got older and the Dickens's domestic Christmases included an increasing number of family and friends, the plays became full-grown theatricals. For these Dickens did not need to use the characters suggested by printed sheets such as *Christmas Gambols and Twelfth Night's Amusements*. He used his own or those of his friend, the novelist Wilkie Collins. Dickens was a seasonal master of ceremonies, whether in person or through his Christmas stories for a vast readership.

The Pickwickian 'traditional' country Christmas at Dingley Dell echoed Irving's in its charm at the time. Part of its original appeal was that, in the golden age of the stagecoach, the reader could imagine the urban-dwelling Pickwickians finding it comparatively easy to travel from the town to the country in the middle of winter. This may seem strange to us, who regard stagecoaches as themselves being part of the nostalgic country Christmas of long ago. But in the late Regency and early Victorian period stagecoaches were viewed very differently. Their increased efficiency at that time, just before the coming of the railways, meant that they were enjoying a golden age. Roads had vastly improved since the mid-eighteenth century: a journey from London to Cambridge that took two days in 1750 was down to seven hours by 1820 and Mr Darcy in *Pride and Prejudice* could confidently declare, 'What is fifty miles of good road? Little more than half a day's journey.' Most importantly, people could and did travel in winter. Thus Parliamentary sittings could now start in the New Year and Lords and Commoners, including country squires like Bracebridge and Wardle, could once again celebrate and entertain at their country estates.

That does not mean that Mr Wardle's Christmas was commonplace, but nostalgia has to be based on possibility, and a stagecoach journey in the snow and a Christmas of the Dingley Dell variety were certainly possible. The images were powerful enough to be integrated by the Victorians into their ideal image of Christmas and, because their ideal is still very much our own, into ours as well.

To this day, Dickens is generally viewed as the author who created that ideal Victorian image. He was also able to describe the annual customs of the smaller-scale urban family Christmas so joyfully and compellingly as to make them part of Christmas tradition. 'Christmas Festivities'* has its own blazing fires, filled glasses, jolly characters, a flaming Christmas pudding and delicious mince pies. It was, like its Pickwickian counterpart, a guide to an enjoyable Christmas for everyone. Or, as Dickens was to stress from 1843 so forcefully, almost everyone…

It was because the image of the new ideal Christmas was so quickly entrenched that Dickens's A Christmas Carol was so powerful. Mr Fezziwig, Scrooge's nephew and even the poor Cratchits all seek to make a 'Merry Christmas'. The unreformed Scrooge does not, but Dickens also points to the ragged, starving children personifying 'Ignorance' and 'Want', who genuinely cannot. For many modern readers (and, of course, viewers), the news that Scrooge is saved is still often followed by the thought, 'Will I be?' It makes A Christmas Carol one of the great secular parables and is the reason it and Dickens himself are a perennial presence in the media every Christmastime.

* Retitled as 'A Christmas Dinner' in Sketches by Boz in 1836.

Queen Victoria's Christmas Tree

....

Prince Albert did not bring the Christmas tree to Britain, as commonly thought, although he certainly gave it a general popularity. It was another royal consort, George III's Queen Charlotte, who introduced a German tradition that was readily taken up by the British aristocracy. The tradition was continued by William IV's Queen Adelaide, herself German born, and in 1832 the future Queen Victoria, then a thirteen-year-old princess, described 'two trees hung with lights and sugar ornaments. All the presents being placed round the tree.'

A December 1848 piece on 'The Christmas Tree at Windsor', in the Christmas supplement of the *Illustrated London News*, showed Victoria and Albert's close family in the best possible light, standing in the magical glow of one of their Christmas trees on Christmas Eve. This child-focused domestic scene sent a calm and reassuring message at the end of a year of revolution across Europe and of political upheaval at home. It also familiarised a wide audience with what Dickens described as 'that pretty German toy, a Christmas tree'.

The article in the *Illustrated London News* gave details of how things were done in the best of homes. Our modern decorated tree can clearly be seen to be a descendant of its royal ancestor:

The tree employed for this festive purpose is a young fir about eight feet high, and has six tiers of branches. On each tier, or branch, are arranged a dozen wax tapers. Pendant from the branches are elegant trays, baskets, bonbonnières,* and other receptacles for sweetmeats, of the most varied and expensive kind; and of all forms, colours and degrees of beauty. Fancy cakes, gilt gingerbread and eggs filled with sweetmeats, are also suspended by variously coloured ribbons from the branches. The tree, which stands upon a table covered with white damask, is supported at the root by piles of sweets of a larger kind, and by toys and dolls of all descriptions, suited to the youthful fancy, and to the several ages of the interesting scions of Royalty for whose gratification they are displayed. The name of each recipient is affixed to the doll, bonbon, or other present intended for it, so that no difference of opinion in the choice of dainties may arise to disturb the equanimity of the illustrious juveniles. On the summit of the tree stands the small figure of an angel, with outstretched wings, holding in each hand a wreath. Those trees are objects of much interest to all visitors at the Castle, from Christmas Eve, when they are first set up, until Twelfth Night, when they are finally removed.

Following Albert's premature death in 1861, Queen Victoria began to spend the Christmas season at Osborne

* Sweet boxes.

'The Christmas Tree' by J. E. Carpenter and Henry Farmer, 1857

House on the Isle of Wight. Influenced by her mourning for Albert, these were much more sober affairs. However, by the 1880s, surrounded by her children and many grandchildren, the Queen allowed much of the gaiety of her earlier Christmases to be restored.

A patriotic Victorian addition for the British family Christmas tree was an adornment of flags. In pride of place, instead of the angel, was the Union Jack.

The first printed illustration of a Christmas tree in the United States also had a German origin. It appeared in 1836 as the frontispiece, entitled 'Christmas Eve', in *The Stranger's Gift* by Hermann Bokum, a German immigrant who taught the German language at Harvard. As for the establishment of the tradition itself in America, it was begun by William Augustus Muhlenberg, the rector of an Episcopalian church in New York who first set up a tree, in his Sunday school, in 1847. The practice very rapidly established itself in the city and the surrounding areas, and it was from there that it was taken nationwide.

Since 1947 the people of Norway have provided a giant Norwegian spruce Christmas tree for London's Trafalgar Square, in gratitude for the UK's support in the Second World War. The lighting ceremony of the tree at New York's Rockefeller Center, normally also a Norwegian spruce, has been a television event since 1964.

The First Christmas Cards and Crackers

....

It is singularly appropriate that London's Victoria & Albert Museum holds the UK's national collection of greetings cards, as Henry Cole, its first director, was also the originator of the first professionally printed commercial Christmas card in 1843.

It was then customary to write letters to send Christmas greetings, but in 1843 Cole found himself short of time. He was a senior and extremely busy civil servant: having already played a key role in the creation of the Penny Post, he would go on to be central to the planning of the Great Exhibition of 1851 and the creation of the museum and cultural district of South Kensington over the subsequent two decades. Cole ingeniously conceived the novel idea of following the tradition of Valentine's cards by producing a printed card for Christmas. He commissioned the well-known artist John Callcott Horsley, approved his design on 17 December 1843, and had the cards printed and delivered, all in time for Christmas. In addition to those printed for friends and acquaintances, others were offered for sale.

The cracker was another invention of the 1840s. Tom Smith, a London confectioner, was pondering how to increase the sales of his wrapped sugar-almond bonbons when he was inspired by the sound of a log crackling on a fire. He decided to create a similar sound for when the

Reproduction of the Christmas card designed by
John Callcott Horsley for Henry Cole in 1843

sweet was unwrapped. Once Smith solved the problem of
creating a harmless minor explosion, the cracker was born.
His innovation was so successful that by 1850 the almond
had been relegated in favour of toys, trinkets and jewellery.
When Smith's son Walter later added the paper crown,
everyone could now become a festive king or queen with
added lucky charms.

Santa Claus As We See Him

....

The figure in 'Old Santeclaus to Much Delight' is in many respects close to the Santa Claus that would eventually capture the public imagination. Yet he lacks some crucial elements of the Santa Claus we know and love today. His birch stick counts against him, as does his priggish tone. The successful Santa Claus would be altogether more benevolent and jovial, but, even then, it would take years for him to assume the dominance in the public imagination that he has now held for more than a century and a half.

In appearance, though not in name, Santa Claus is famously described fully fledged for the very first time in 'A Visit from St Nicholas', a poem perhaps better known through its first line as 'The Night Before Christmas'. Its creator, Clement Clarke Moore, certainly knew Washington Irving and his work. He might well have known the anonymous poem 'Old Santeclaus with Much Delight' and its illustrations, and has even been suggested as its author, though, bearing in mind the completely different tone of 'The Night Before Christmas' just a year after, that might be thought surprising.

Moore initially wrote 'The Night Before Christmas' in 1822, as merely a diversion for his children, and he was furious when a supposed friend published it anonymously on his behalf the following year. However, Moore did later acknowledge ownership and several times amended the names of his seventh and eighth reindeer – though the final stage in their move from Dunder and Blixem (colloquial New York Dutch for thunder and lightning) to Donner and Blitzen (their equivalent in German) only came in the early twentieth century, well after Moore's death.

The German-born Thomas Nast was a brilliant and highly influential political cartoonist: indeed, he has been described as the father of modern political cartooning in the United States. He was also the artist who, over time, refined the elfin St Nicholas of Moore's poem and portrayed the 'larger-than-life' Santa Claus that is still with us.

Nast's very first image, on the cover of the *Harper's Weekly* Christmas issue for 1862,* shows a solemn Santa, dressed in the Stars and Stripes, in a Union Camp during the American Civil War. However, by the Christmas 1866 issue, Nast was showing an altogether friendlier Santa. In 'Santa Claus: His Works', he was not only delivering toys but making them.

Like Moore before him, Nast was 'creating' the Santa Claus figure with his own young children in mind, though unlike Moore, he was not shy of bringing back the traditional birch in some of his earlier drawings. However, in just a few years Nast had settled on the round, jolly and benevolent figure in the fur-lined-and-trimmed red suit.

It was Nast who gave Santa Claus a mystical home at the North Pole, but he also showed him as a nineteenth-

* Post-dated 3 January 1863.

'Merry Old Santa Claus', illustration by Thomas Nast, 1881

century contemporary figure using the telephone, just as Haddon Sundblom and Norman Rockwell would show Santa in the twentieth century drinking Coca-Cola.

Moore's poem and Nast's illustration (with 'Santa Claus: His Works') appeared together for the first time in 1869, and Moore was the obvious inspiration for Nast's general depiction. Yet there would also be a further change to Santa's identity, as his image travelled east across the Atlantic over the next two decades. Father Christmas as the personification of the Christmas festival had been represented in many different coats of different colours in previous decades, but now his representative coat was definitively red. The reason was made clear in the introduction to Nast's collection of Christmas drawings published in 1890, which described the artist's depiction as 'the bluff, honest Santa Claus of "The Night Before Christmas" … the Santa Claus of unsuspecting childhood … His Santa Claus is old Father Christmas himself.'

Whether he was called Santa Claus in America or Father Christmas in the UK, there could be no doubt that the two were now, most definitively, one and the same.

The Art of Present-Giving

Roman Saturnalia was a time of present-giving to family, friends, slaves and – most certainly – either to people you wished to influence higher up the social hierarchy or those, lower down the scale, whose good service you depended upon. If one was in any doubt, it was better to err on the side of gift-giving and to spend as much as one could. Lucian, in setting out the festival's rules for present-giving in the second century AD, stated that a rich man should be prepared to spend a tenth of his annual income and, in addition, he should give away spare clothes and 'such ware as is too coarse for his own service'. However, Lucian depicted the priest Cronosolon as seeing a need for balance, and advocated that any poor man should be severely beaten if he gave presents that were way beyond his means.

Getting the right balance for work-related present-giving has been a perpetual problem, with the first-century poet Martial's, 'I hate the crafty and mischievous arts of presents,' chiming with Jonathan Swift's eighteenth-century lament, 'I shall be undone here with Christmas boxes.' However, the modern era's increasingly impersonal relationship between suppliers and customers has greatly decreased the custom. As for the seasonal 'present' within firms – the alcohol-fuelled and potentially perilous office party – that, where it continues, has become more restrained in recent years.

For family and friends, present-giving has settled on different days down the centuries and has included New

Year's Day, Twelfth Night and Epiphany (or Twelfth Day).
Clement Clarke Moore moved his St Nicholas's present-
giving from the Saint's name day to Christmas Eve, though
in much of Europe presents are given on both days. Yet
as the years roll by, the growing ubiquity of Santa Claus
and the domestication of Christmas has concentrated the
present-giving into thirty-six hours or so over Christmas
Eve and Christmas Day.

As for the period of potential present-buying, that
has become an exponentially longer process since the
time Victorian shopkeepers first seized the commercial
opportunities offered by Christmas's elevation into a time
for ritualised goodwill and hospitality. The world of the
stagecoach might be idealised on Christmas cards, but it
was the more integrated world of the railway that gave
firms greater regional and national reach and the equivalent
newspapers and magazines in which to advertise their
wares. Thus, by the 1880s, the large department stores were
already competing with each other to provide stunning
Christmas window displays to entice their customers.

In Victorian times, some of the working families without
access to banks would save for their Christmas dinner by
contributing a small sum each week to a 'goose club'. But
Christmas could also be, in the words of Dickens's Scrooge,
'a time for paying bills without money', with the New Year
supplying a harsh reality.

Illustration by John Pimlott for *The Sphere*, 28 November 1932

THE SPHERE

"I sneaked in," whispered the child,
"because I wanted to see you special.
Because you're Santa Claus, and you
can get a kid anything what he wants.
Can't you?" "Why, yes, youngster,"
Alan said, trying to sound convincing

Santa's Christmas Presence

Thomas Nast's enduring image gave artistic form to the Anglo-American creation that is Santa Claus. The subsequent physical presence in department stores was another Anglo-American joint effort.

Though there are a number of store Santas who could be said to be the first to don the red outfit, the best documented is James Edgar, the Scottish-born owner of a department store in Brockton, Massachusetts, who, in 1890, decided to walk around the store dressed as Nast's Santa Claus. It seems that Edgar had no commercial intent in mind, but was merely fond of dressing up and wanted to entertain children and to promote Christmas. However, within days, families travelled by train from Boston and from as far afield as Providence, Rhode Island to see him.

This real live Nast Santa was quickly copied in stores on both sides of the Atlantic and may on occasion have displaced other Christmas figures.

'Father Christmas distributes presents to children in a department store', illustration by Jay Hyde Barnum for *Good Housekeeping*, December 1932

Boxing Day and the New Year

In the religious calendar, 26 December is the feast day of St Stephen, the first Christian martyr. It was on this day that, in the carol, 'Good King Wenceslas went out'.

However 26 December is now generally better known as Boxing Day. The term stems from the time when the good service of tradesmen and performance of servants was rewarded by their customers or employers with a Christmas-box gift, often of money.

From the early nineteenth century onwards, Boxing Day has also been considered a great day for sporting activity, a time for the healthy outdoors and exercise after a day of excess calories and of being closeted indoors with family. Activity on horseback is particularly appropriate on that day, with St Stephen being the patron saint of horses.

New Year's Eve has taken over Twelfth Night's position as the night of revelry. Twelfth Night's importance dwindled during the nineteenth century with the urbanised industrial economy cutting down the English twelve days of Christmas to three, including the day itself and the two on either side. Even then Boxing Day was only recognised as a bank holiday within the English Christmas season by an 1871 Act of Parliament. Although 26 December is not a public holiday in the United States, many people, as in the UK and Europe, use the time between Christmas Eve and the early

'Auld Lang Syne' illustration by John Massey Wright, 1842

92

New Year for an extended break. In fact, should Christmas Eve fall on a Monday and be taken as leave and 2 January also be included (as it naturally is in Scotland, to recover from Hogmanay) then a modern 'Twelve Days of Christmas' is created.

With Hogmanay, the Scots have traditionally made much more of the New Year than the English. Hogmanay, rather than Christmas, had been the Scots' midwinter festival right up to the 1950s. It was only then that Christmas Day, for the first time in 400 years, became a holiday again in Scotland – with Boxing Day joining it in the 1970s. Hogmanay sees the tradition of 'first footing', where a tall, dark-haired 'stranger' delivers symbolic pieces of coal, shortbread, salt, black bun and the all-important wee dram of whisky and steps over the threshold to usher in the New Year. In contrast to England, where there was no formal New Year's Day holiday until the 1970s, the seriousness of the Scottish celebrations entitles the Scots to take the first two days of the New Year as holiday.

Pantomime

....

In terms of its popular appeal, our pantomime is a worthy descendant of the mumming, wassailing and other performing activities extolled in masques by Ben Jonson and later condemned by the Puritans. It is no less than a tamed modern version of the world turned upside down, with its irreverence, bawdy jokes (coded for adult enjoyment) and substantial cross-dressing.

Pantomime's roots stretch back to Saturnalia and beyond to Ancient Greece. The word 'pantomime' derives both from the Ancient Greek *pantomimos*, 'imitator of all' and from the Latin *pantomimus*, for an actor using mime.

The origins of the English pantomime lie in the Italian *commedia dell'arte*, a type of spoken street theatre known to Shakespeare, whose own comedies such as *Twelfth Night* feature cross-dressing and chaotic misunderstandings. In 1717 John Rich, a London impresario, adapted the form to suit his own talents as a dancer, acrobat and mime artist, and produced a spectacle of magic, cross-dressing and humans dressed as animals. His performances over the next thirty-five years were so popular with their rowdy audiences that pantomimes were seen as a vulgar threat both to public order and to serious theatre. With the latter in mind, David Garrick, the eighteenth century's greatest actor-impresario, contrived to get them restricted to the Christmas season.

The next great heyday of the pantomime came in the first quarter of the nineteenth century, due to Joseph Grimaldi, the son of an Italian immigrant father who was himself a London pantomime actor from the late 1750s to the 1780s. Beginning as a child, Grimaldi junior had been in pantomime for almost twenty years before he took the role of the clown in 1800. He began transforming the clown to become the star of the show and developed what Dickens (who watched Grimaldi as a child, and later edited his memoirs) described as 'a stupendous phenomenon' of riotous stage activity, of locking up policemen and stealing everything in sight. Grimaldi combined frenetic mime, comic song and linking stage patter but did so with an underlying seam of pathos.

That last element was, in the late Victorian period, to form part of the character of the pantomime dame. There was certainly riotousness all round, but the dame was law-abiding and down on her luck. Once again, one man took a marginal character in the dame, and made it the main one. From the 1880s to the turn of the century, the Irish actor known as Dan Leno both created the role and was its most famous performer. He set a style and standard for the pantomime that lasted well into the television age.

In the current century, 'celebrity' stars of TV soaps and even sports have entered panto and, in many cases, the principal boy/girl and even the dame have exited the stage. Some see this as showing that a great and very British institution is dying, but, considering its very mutability, the answer to that can only be, 'Oh, no it isn't!'

Poster for the pantomime at Theatre Royal, Drury Lane, 1890

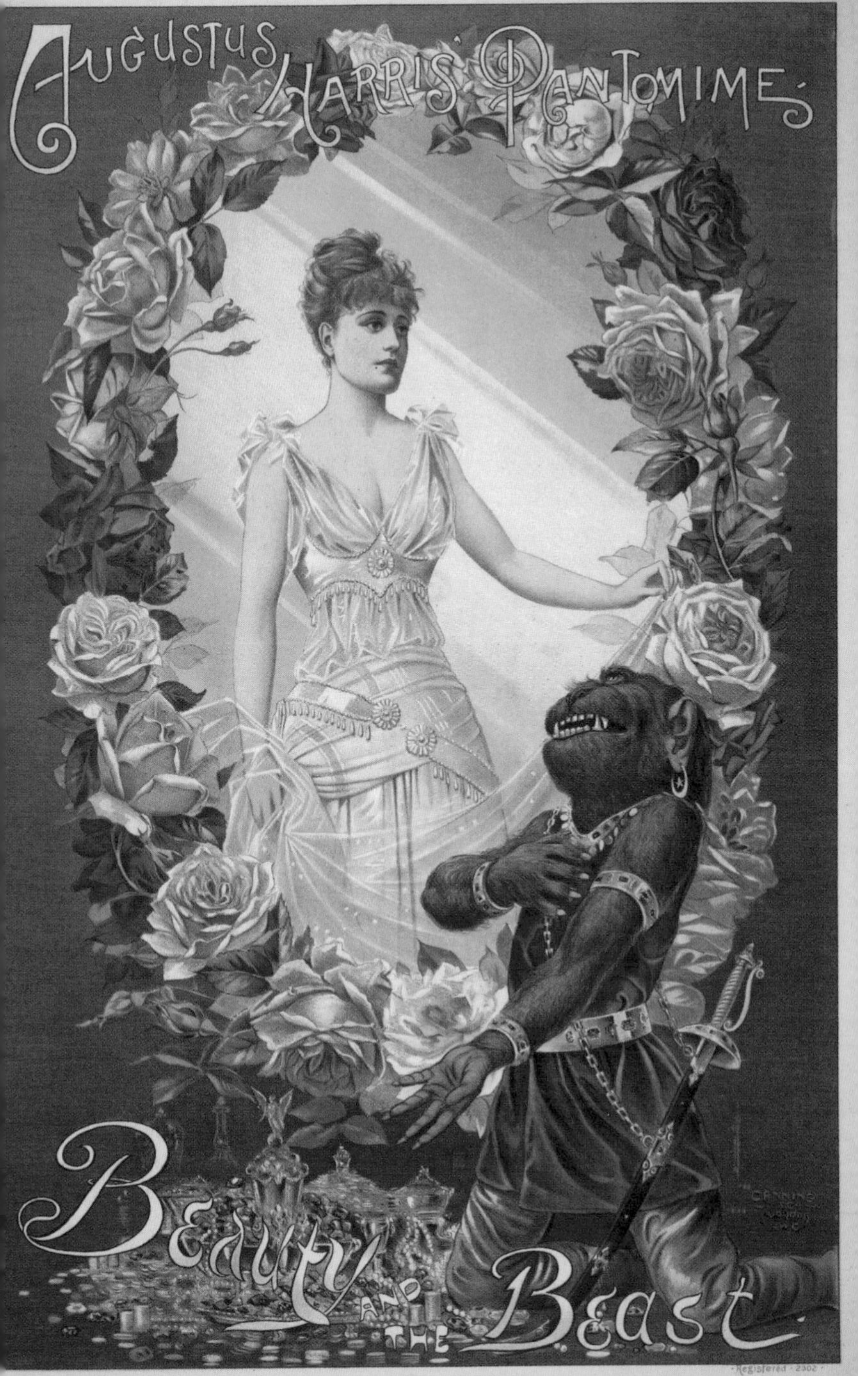

· Registered · 2302 ·

CHRISTMAS
AROUND THE
World

Japan

. . . .

Over the past century and a half, Christmas has become the world's pre-eminent midwinter festival. Many of the 'traditional' features in today's European and American celebrations are adaptations of ancient local customs or valued modern additions. The contemporary transatlantic Christmas has successfully travelled across the world with a universally joyful central message and forms of celebration that can blend with established local traditions and also create new ones. The results can be startling and imaginative, with Japan providing excellent examples.

As the previous illustration shows, the nineteenth-century Santa Claus was recognised in Japan by at least 1914. Christmas began to feature more widely after the Second World War, with department stores competing with lights and decorations to take advantage of its commercial aspect. Though not a public holiday, Christmas in Japan has its own customs. For instance, it has become traditional to eat takeaway fried chicken on Christmas Day and Japan has its own Christmas cake, which is a light sponge covered in whipped cream and decorated with strawberries.

The Japanese New Year, Shōgatsu, is the time for family celebration. In contrast, Christmas Day today is more likely to be an adult romantic occasion, more akin to the Western St Valentine's Day.

Germany

The Anglo-Saxon and Viking midwinter traditions of our distant past and the nineteenth-century popularity of the decorated Christmas tree both have their roots in northern Europe and Scandinavia. The Christmas market (Christkindlmarkt) is becoming the latest continental Christmas tradition to establish itself in Britain and North America. These markets have a long history in Germany and Austria, particularly if their medieval antecedents are considered. Dresden has the oldest specifically described Christmas market, which dates back to 1434.

The run-up to the German Christmas begins with Advent and is marked with a special wreath displayed in homes and churches as well as by the Advent calendar. Most Christmas markets also start at around this time and continue to Christmas Eve or just before. As well as having stalls selling handicrafts and decorations that are particularly appropriate for Christmas and the season of present-giving, the larger Christmas markets can have choirs and funfair rides for children, as well as a huge variety of things to eat to accompany the Glühwein.

Among the great number of seasonal sweet things are biscuits, cakes such as Stollen, and all manner of items made of gingerbread, of which the most complex and impressive are the gingerbread houses.

Like much of continental Europe, many Germans celebrate the visit of St Nicholas on the eve or day of

6 December and have their major Christmas celebrations on Christmas Eve.

In a piece accompanying their description of the royal Christmas tree in 1848, the *Illustrated London News* told their readers of an established German tradition. This referred to the adults' decoration of the family tree after sunset on Christmas Eve, with the children kept fully occupied elsewhere. Along with ornaments and sweets, the tree is described as being festooned with candles to be lit moments before the children are called to see the display. This charming tradition, long-standing then, continues to this day.

(pages 98–9) Japanese illustration of Santa Claus, from *Kodomo no tomo* (*The Children's Companion*), 1914

(left) Moriz Jung, *Merry Christmas! (Frohe Weihnachten!)*, colour lithograph, 1907

Scandinavia

....

One of the striking elements of the Swedish Christmas is the Feast of St Lucia, which begins the Christmas season on 13 December. St Lucia fed the starving during a famine and her day is commemorated by the eldest daughter of the family, as the 'Lucia Bride', serving her parents breakfast in bed with coffee and special saffron buns. The Lucia Bride, dressed in white, inaugurates the new season by wearing a crown of evergreens with seven lighted candles. For safety reasons, the 'candles' these days are most often battery-operated candle lights, which is partly the reason that in modern Denmark the tradition has been taken up and adapted for schools with a St Lucia leading a singing procession.

In the same way that the gift-giving Santa Claus is Father Christmas in the UK, so he is also now Julemand (Yule Man) in Denmark and Jultomten in Sweden. The difference between the two Scandinavian figures is that in Sweden the gift giver is also the household elf, whereas in Denmark the gift-giving Julemand and the elfin Julenisse are separate figures, with the latter's natural mischief-making kept at bay through seasonal offerings of rice porridge.

The Swedes' main meal on Christmas Eve is a smorgasbord of meat and fish dishes, now more sensible in its quantities than the feasts of old. They do though still commemorate the famine days of yesteryear with the tradition of dipping pieces of bread in the water in which a ham has been boiled.

Though St Knut was a Danish king, it is not in his own country but in Sweden that his saint's day, 13 January, is important, as it marks the end of the Christmas season. This is the time when children rifle the Christmas tree for its remaining treats and a final party is held. In Denmark, Christmas ends on Three Kings' Day, 6 January.

Norway, which had been in unions both with Denmark and Sweden before going its separate way in 1904, shares many of the customs of its neighbours. This includes the Scandinavian version of the King of Bean: whoever finds the hidden almond in their Christmas porridge is deemed lucky and will, according to different traditions, either receive a small prize or can expect to have luck for the next year.

'St Lucia's Day', illustration from *Allers Familj-Journal*, 1927

Mexico

....

Many of the Mexican Christmas traditions date back to the sixteenth century and were introduced by Spanish missionaries intent on subsuming Aztec practices. The Christmas season's first event, the Feast of the Virgen de Guadalupe (Mexico's patron saint), takes place on 12 December. This is when the Christmas markets open and begin selling seasonal food and fruit punch.

The nine nights of Las Posadas begin on 16 December, when a child dressed as an angel leads two others who hold clay images of Mary and Joseph. They are at the head of a singing procession through the streets and, after being ritually turned away by 'innkeepers' at the first houses they try, they are admitted at the last. All the children then gather together to sing carols at that house's Nacimiento (Nativity scene) and to have a meal and play games, including smashing star-shaped clay or papier-mâché piñatas for the sweets and treats inside them. A different family hosts each evening, when model figures are added to each Nacimiento. On the ninth night, Nochebuena (Christmas Eve), the last of the model figures are produced and everyone involved has their big Christmas party with fireworks.

The traditional day for giving presents is Epiphany, not Christmas Day, with the Three Kings filling the children's stockings. However, with Santa Claus continually adding to his devotees worldwide, for some lucky children there is a second stocking-filling over Christmas.

Christmas in Mexico: breaking the piñata, early twentieth-century photograph

Seasonal Present-Bringers

....

Santa Claus's popularity as a present-bringer has gradually eclipsed that of all others since the 1870s. In some places, Santa Claus and the longer-established national gift-giver have become one and the same white-bearded man in a red outfit. This has been the case with Father Christmas in the UK, Père Noël in France, the Weihnachtsmann in Germany and, as has been mentioned, their equivalents in Scandinavia. Santa Claus may be more recent in his creation than these European figures, but his precursor, St Nicholas, is far older than all of them. What brought his temporary eclipse and the opportunity for the others was the Reformation.

The opposition of the new Protestant movements to Catholic devotion to saints increased during the sixteenth century and St Nicholas, for one, was banned. Christmas celebrations were also far more muted, but in a number of cases the present-bringing tradition continued or was revived. Thus, for example, in some Protestant areas of Germany, Switzerland and the Hapsburg Empire, St Nicholas was replaced by the Christkindl or Christ Child. Initially baby Jesus was claimed as this present-giver, but the Christkindl soon changed into an angelic figure in white, complete with wand and golden crown. Martin Luther himself was happy for St Nicholas and the Christkindl to coexist, but later reformers such as John Calvin proscribed the saint. The Christkindl still survives today, but is perhaps best known as the name for the German-style Christmas market – Christkindlmarkt – and for Kris Kringle in America, now just a pseudonym there for Santa Claus.

In some Christian countries – whether Protestant, Catholic or Orthodox – a pre-existing present-bringer has survived alongside Santa Claus. That survival was made all the easier where the two gift-givers have different delivery days, as children are always likely to prefer two days of presents to just one.

In Italy, the national present-giver is La Befana, an old woman whose name is a corruption of 'Epiphania', who visits after dark on 5 January, the eve of Epiphany. La Befana's story is a sad one: she delayed joining the Magi (the Wise Men) on their journey to Bethlehem and thus, to her everlasting regret, she missed the chance of seeing the Christ Child and has searched for him ever since. With this in mind, it might be thought unsurprising that the Christmas Eve visits of the altogether jollier Italian Babbo Natale (literally 'Daddy Christmas') are increasingly popular – particularly, as with the original American Sinterklaas, La Befana threatens to bring something less than welcome to bad children, which in her case is seemingly lumps of coal or a bagful of ashes. However, these days the black lumps (for both good and 'bad' children) are sweets and, in many towns and villages across Italy, communal bonfires on the eve of Epiphany or on the day itself bring an enjoyable end to the Christmas season. La Befana's exact Russian equivalent, in terms of her wanderings, is Baboushka.

Washington Irving's gentle satire began the American

transformation of Sinterklaas, the Dutch St Nicholas, into Santa Claus. Yet, as Sinterklaas in the Netherlands, St Nicholas in Belgium and the Kleeschen in Luxembourg, he continues to bring presents and fill stockings for his saint's day. He has a particularly high profile in the Netherlands, even though, with his previous existence curtailed by the Reformation, his modern incarnation only dates from the mid-nineteenth century. The reborn Sinterklaas was then given a helper in the form of Zwarte (Black) Piet from Africa, who took over the birch-carrying duties. More recently, Piet has himself been transformed and is now often the soot-blackened Chimney Piet, who only delivers nice presents. Every year Sinterklaas arrives by boat from his home in Spain a full three weeks before his name day and his arrival is a major televised event. Then, by 7 December, with his work completed, he leaves the way clear for the Kerstman, his Santa-Claus-styled alter ego.

In his embodiment as the jolly, round, white-bearded man in the red suit, Santa Claus may be comparatively new; but, as the festive spirit of giving at the darkest time of year, he is clearly identifiable as a modern, if secular, version of ancient St Nicholas. His ever-increasing international recognition and rise in popularity since the nineteenth century has echoed that of the festival of Christmas itself.

'La Befana', illustration from Le Magasin pittoresque, 1840
(next pages) The White House takes on Christmas dress, Washington, D.C., 19 December 1939

RUDOLPH

THE RED-NOSED
REINDEER

Written for

MONTGOMERY WARD

by

ROBERT L. MAY

Author of "Benny the Bunny Liked Beans"

ILLUSTRATED BY DENVER GILLEN

Rudolph Lights the Way

....

Santa's story, like his sleigh, found its guiding light in 1939, when Rudolph belatedly joined the reindeer team. Rudolph the Red-Nosed Reindeer had a completely commercial genesis. Rudolph's Santa-saving feat first appeared as a much longer story in a holiday-season children's colouring book distributed by the Montgomery Ward department stores, then the USA's largest retailer. It was written at their Chicago HQ by an in-house copywriter called Robert L. May, with the firm giving away 2.5 million copies in 1939 and a reprint in 1946 taking the total up to 6 million.

In 1947 Montgomery Ward's CEO gave May the copyright and in 1949 May's brother-in-law, Johnny Marks, wrote the famous song. It was not immediately taken up and then only as a B-side on a single by Gene Autry, 'the singing cowboy'. Yet it was Rudolph that captured the American public's imagination as the Christmas week number-one hit, selling 2.5 million that year alone, and it is second only to Irving Berlin and Bing Crosby's 'White Christmas' as the bestselling Christmas record of all time.

Rudolph has since been a multimedia sensation, appearing in films and on TV – even in Dr Who – as well as being a regular on Christmas cards. The song, along with 'White Christmas', is at the beginning of a long line of secular novelty Christmas records that first dominate the charts and then join the popular canon.

Title page to *Rudolph the Red-Nosed Reindeer*, 1939

The Royal Christmas

The first royal Christmas Day broadcast was given over the radio by George V in 1932. Using text written by Rudyard Kipling, the King spoke for two and a half minutes at 3 p.m. GMT on Christmas Day, and his voice was relayed to much of the British Empire. The broadcast was established as an annual event during the Second World War and George VI's words were considered extremely effective in raising morale.

Queen Elizabeth II's first radio broadcast, from the same desk at Sandringham used by her father and grandfather, was in 1952. The first televised Queen's Speech was in 1957, and the first time it was recorded was in 1960, when tapes sent to the countries of the Commonwealth allowed it to be aired at the most suitable local time.

Today, the Christmas Day broadcast is an occasion when the monarch chooses the theme and speaks to the public directly. It retains its traditional UK television time of 3 p.m. but is also available across the full range of modern media.

As to the Queen's own traditions, since 1988 the Royal Family have celebrated Christmas and New Year at the Queen's Sandringham estate in Norfolk. The family exchange presents at teatime on Christmas Eve and attend the morning service at the local church of St Mary Magdalene on Christmas Day.

All members of the Royal Household receive a present from the Queen and she continues another tradition of her father and grandfather in funding the distribution of 1,500 Christmas puddings.

As well as having her own trees at Christmas, the Queen donates trees to Westminster Abbey and St Paul's Cathedral in London, to St Giles' Cathedral and the Canongate Kirk in Edinburgh, and to churches and schools close to Sandringham.

'The King's Christmas Message to His Subjects', *Weekly Illustrated*, 21 December 1935

White House Christmases

Whether US presidents emphasise the word 'Christmas' or the multi-faith phrase of 'Holiday Season', or use the phrases interchangeably, the White House's own examples show how traditions can develop over a century.

It was President Calvin Coolidge who first pushed the button to light up the National Community Christmas Tree in 1923. In 1924, and for most years in the following decades, the ceremony was held in an area of the President's Park just south of the White House. However, it is only since 1954 that it has had its permanent home there.

Initially the lighting ceremony happened on Christmas Eve, but in 1954 the organisers made it part of a wider Christmas Pageant of Peace celebration of nightly events, and it expanded during the following decades to become a regular three-week festival.

The 'Pathway of Peace' of smaller trees that represent all the American states and territories and the District of Columbia itself first appeared in 1954. Since 1981 the Pathway trees have been decorated with ornaments from the areas they represent and from 2008 it has had a Santa's workshop.

Inside the White House it is now traditional to have a Christmas tree in the Blue Room. The first time one appeared there was in 1912, and the tradition of having an annual theme was created by First Lady Jacqueline

Calvin Coolidge and the National Community Christmas Tree, 1923

Kennedy in 1961. In their turn, the White House Historical Association has designed a new official ornament each year since 1981.

There are a number of other decorative elements that have become established as Christmas perennials. One such is the gingerbread house. It started with the Johnson family and a gingerbread cottage on the table in front of the mirror in the State Dining Room in 1968 and was followed by the Nixons with an A-shaped gingerbread house the following year. Since then, White House chefs have made a succession of elaborate buildings. From the 1990s they have most often featured the White House itself, which on occasion has become a white chocolate White House.

It is ironic that the tradition of the broadcast Christmas message was also started by the notoriously taciturn Calvin Coolidge. As President Harding was caring for his convalescing wife in the White House, it was Vice President Coolidge who, on 13 December 1922, recorded the radio message for Christmas Eve. More recently the First Lady has joined the President in recording a televised goodwill message.

The Modern Advent Calendar

....

The modern advent calendar is another Christmas tradition that has come to Britain from Germany. In this case both the German original and the British imported version are comparatively recent.

Advent, spreading over the four Sundays before Christmas, is for Christians a time of anticipation and preparation. During the nineteenth century in Germany the method of counting down the days changed from chalk marks on doors and the lighting of small candles to making homemade Advent calendars. It was not until the early twentieth century that these calendars were printed, with their windows, which when opened illustrated the Christmas story in pictures and verse.

The Advent calendar was first introduced into the UK and America after the Second World War, and President Eisenhower and his grandchildren boosted their popularity as part of a campaign for charity.

The modern-style calendar does not keep to the Advent timetable, but provides a twenty-four-day countdown to Christmas with the old-style verses giving way to chocolates and sweets. That version is now also available in Germany.

Lights and Garlands

....

From time immemorial, our ancestors in the northern hemisphere have sought to mark midwinter, when days are at their shortest and nature at its most dormant, by looking forward to the lengthening of days and the approach of spring. One part of this celebration of things to come has been the gathering of evergreens and their combination with pressed flowers in wreaths and garlands; another has been the use of light, both as an added bonus to the warmth of fires or as a benefit in itself. Lights and garlands, both separately or together, were deployed within the decorative setting for Saturnalia and Yule. The same is true of Christmas.

The Advent wreath tells us of the coming of Christmas. It was originally a Lutheran custom, but has spread more widely. On each of the four Sundays in Advent an additional candle on the wreath is lit, with, in some traditions, a fifth placed in the centre to be lit on Christmas Eve or Christmas Day. Another combination of lights and greenery is, of course, the Christmas tree.

Part of the appeal of Christmastime is that it gives adults the opportunity to pass on to their children and grandchildren the seasonal rituals handed down to them by their own parents and grandparents. They also can, and do, introduce new ones, which the children will pass to future generations and which will soon become an essential part of the traditional celebration of Christmas.

Christmas trees and Blickling Hall lit up during the evening
at Blickling Estate, Norfolk

Heritage organisations add to the enjoyment of
Christmastime by presenting reimagined Christmases of
the past in the settings of the period. Thus the National
Trust, the UK's largest heritage charity, can offer a full range,
from the medieval (including wassailing) right through
to domestic Christmases of the various decades of the
twentieth century. But, as a sign that the new traditions
of Christmas can be creative embellishments of age-
old themes, the Trust also offers popular community
events such as Christmas light shows and wreath-making
– including the giant sixty-foot garland at Cotehele in
Cornwall, itself a tradition that has grown since 1956.

Afterword

The great joy of Christmas is that although its traditions are always changing, even the newer ones soon gain a vintage quality that renders them timeless – and particularly so for children.

One cannot say for how long Santa Claus and Christmas turkey will retain the pre-eminence they have gained over the last century and a half. Perhaps we should not dismiss the current fad of decorating family dogs to look like reindeer, or the newly ubiquitous Christmas-jumper parties; maybe these in their turn will become traditions.

However, whether Christmas is to be enjoyed primarily as a religious or secular occasion, everyone in the northern hemisphere must surely agree with the benevolent if old-fashioned Sir Roger de Coverley, that 'it happens very well that Christmas should fall out in the Middle of Winter'.

The final words should go to Dickens, whose vision of the Victorian urban Christmas still retains its power as *the* traditional Christmas. As Dickens wrote in 'A Christmas Dinner', the first of his stories about the festive season: 'There seems a magic in the very name of Christmas.'

Decorating the Christmas tree, illustration by R. Beyschlag from *Gartenlaube*, 1892

Further Reading

....

Timothy Larsen (ed.), *The Oxford Handbook of Christmas* (forthcoming, 2021)

Gerry Bowler, *The World Encyclopaedia of Christmas* (2000)
— *Santa Claus: A Biography* (2005)
— *Christmas in the Crosshairs* (2016)

Alan Davidson and Tom Jaine, *The Oxford Companion to Food* (third edition, 2014)

Percy Dearmer, *The Oxford Book of Carols* (1974)

Charles Dickens, 'Christmas Festivities', retitled in *Sketches by Boz* (1836) as 'A Christmas Dinner'
— *The Pickwick Papers* (1837)
— *A Christmas Carol* (1843)

Mark Forsyth, *A Christmas Cornucopia: The Hidden Stories Behind Our Yuletide Traditions* (2016)

J. M. Golby and A. W. Purdue, *The Making of the Modern Christmas* (2000)

Lucinda Hawksley, *Dickens and Christmas* (2017)

Ronald Hutton, *The Stations of the Sun: A History of the Ritual Year in Britain* (1996)

Washington Irving, *A History of New-York* (1809)
— *The Sketch Book of Geoffrey Crayon, Gent.* (1819–20)

Alison Latham, *The Oxford Companion to Music* (2011)

Stephen Nissenbaum, *The Battle for Christmas* (1997)

Jacqueline Simpson and Steve Roud, *A Dictionary of English Folklore* (2003)

Michael Stephenson, *The Christmas Almanac* (1992)

Christopher Winn, *The Book of Christmas* (2018)

www.georgegoodwin.com

Acknowledgements

....

It is no wonder that the works of Timothy Larsen and
Gerry Bowler are so prominent in this book's further
reading list. Their books alone would merit them having first
place in my acknowledgements, but these great experts on
the history of Christmas have also been personally helpful
to me.

Tim Travis at the V&A, which houses the national
collection of cards for all occasions, happily dealt with my
query about Christmas cards, and among the others who
have assisted me more generally are Christopher Winn,
Chantry Westwell, Gerry Bodily and Jerry White.

My thanks to John Lee and Rob Davies at British Library
Publishing for taking up my suggestion for the book, to Liz
Woabank (who has guided the project throughout) and to
Kate Quarry, Sally Nicholls, Maria Vassilopoulos, Catherine
Best and Briony Hartley, who have seen it to completion
and beyond. I am greatly indebted to the British Library's
Eccles Centre for American Studies – Phil Hatfield, Cara
Rodway, Philip Abraham and Jean Petrovic – both for their
support for me with a Makin Fellowship, but also for getting
the book better known, along with the Anglo-American
origins of so many of the modern Christmas festivities.

Finally I would like to thank my own family, in particular
my late mother-in-law, for making Christmas such a special
time for our own household in Kew.

Credits

....

All illustrations are from the collections of the
British Library unless otherwise stated.

First published 2019 by
The British Library
96 Euston Road
London NW1 2DB

British Library Cataloguing in Publication Data

A catalogue record for this publication is available
from the British Library

ISBN 978 0 7123 5294 9

Designed by Goldust Design
Picture research by Sally Nicholls

Printed and bound in
FINIDR, Czech Republic